Contents

Using the Classroom Resources

This pack has been designed for use by GCSE, VCE, AS and A2 level Media Studies teachers and students. The practical tasks, written and research exercises that are included aim to foster and facilitate group work, practical and creative skills, and the critical autonomy of individual students. All of these tasks/exercises can be differentiated according to group needs and abilities.

The Classroom Resources are divided into two main sections: the first section asks students to look at the way 'old media' such as film, television, and popular music have been transformed by new media technologies; and the second section asks students to critically assess the impact of three new media technologies - the Internet, electronic gaming, and DV camera surveillance - on the modern world. The author hopes that such investigations will not only lead to a celebration of the new media but a critical appraisal of its more negative effects on people today. Although designed for stand-alone use, the teacher will benefit most from using these resources in conjunction with **The New Media: A Teacher's Guide**, which is also available from Auteur Publishing.

The New Media and the Modern World

What are the New Media?

The new media are those media technologies and media forms that are historically recent in terms of invention, entry into the marketplace, and into everyday use.

Working in pairs

Here is a the list of some of the most important new media technologies that have entered the home in recent years:

Home Computer	*PlayStation (2) console*
MiniDisc player	Digital TV
Digital camcorder	*Internet enabled mobile phone*
Synthesiser	GameBoy
DVD player	

1. Mentally tick off the ones you are familiar with, or know most about, and begin to think about the benefits and/or the pleasures that each of these new media technologies have brought their users.

    Make written notes if this helps you to remember what you have discussed.

2. Narrow your selection down to just *two* from the above list.

Produce (design) a magazine or newspaper article that describes how these two new media technologies have transformed the way the media (they are associated with) are transmitted and received in the home. To help you with this think about these general areas:

Sound and picture quality	Channel and programme choice
Portability and mobility	*Communication*
Information gathering	Creativity and interactivity
Role play and escapism	*Privacy*
Special effects	Immediacy

What are the New Media? II

New media texts are supposedly marked by *real interactivity*, an abundance of *special effects*, an *increase in visual stimulation*, and by an *exhilarating speed* in delivery.

One only has to think of the development of broadband technology on the Internet for the way it has supposedly brought about the real-time streaming of high quality video and audio accelerated connection speeds (up to 40 times faster than standard dial-up connections), making interactivity between users instantaneous.

Research Task

In groups of 3 or 4

1. Use your School or College's Internet to carry out the following tasks, timing how long it takes you to complete them (start the clock for task 1 the moment you begin to log on).

   - Search for and download a picture of Tony Blair.

   - Email the picture of Tony Blair to someone from another group.

   - Search for, download, and watch all the way through a recently released film trailer.

   - Search for and download a piece of music that is either outside of copyright restrictions or which has been put on the Web by the record company.

   - Search for listings on global warming. Visit 3 of the Web sites listed and print off their homepages.

2. How quickly did you, could you complete these tasks? Was 'downloading' a slow process? If so, how might you want to amend the definition of the new media given above?

Now produce your own 4 sentence definition of the new media.

1.3

What are the New Media? III

The new media are often technological innovations or radical transformations of existing ('old') media and communication technologies. For example:

- *Television* has been transformed by digital and satellite technology.
- *Game console playing* has been transformed by DVD and Internet.
- *Listening to music* has been transformed by CD, the personal stereo, the mini-disc and MTV.
- *Films* have been transformed by special effects and CGI (computer generated imagery).

In groups of 3 or 4

1. Choose what you collectively think are the five most important media inventions of the last ten years. Rank them in order of importance and then present your list, and the reasons behind your decisions, to the rest of the class.

    Visual or audio-visual support (acetates, video clips, flip chart) should be part of the presentation.

    Use the library and the Internet to help you research your chosen media inventions.

2. Collectively, try to make a prediction of how one media technology may be advanced or improved in the future. Share your ideas with the rest of the class.

The New Media and the Visualisation of Culture

Over the course of the twentieth century the mass media developed from one being dependent on the written word (*reading*) and on sound (*hearing*) to one being dependent on vision (*seeing*). The shift in dominance from the press and radio to film, advertising and television is a shift based on privileging one sense - sight - above all others.

(Task)

1.   *A Day in my Visual World*

      Describe or draw a picture-collage of a *day in your life* in terms of all the visual media, visual technologies that you come into contact with. Use this list to help you:

      TV, DVD, CD-ROM; Internet; newspapers and magazines; posters; album/CD/DVD/video covers; still and moving adverts; billboards; gaming consoles; surveillance cameras; camcorders; stills cameras; photo albums; bus passes; road signs, etc.

2.   How important do you think the new media have been to making the world feel like it is increasingly experienced visually - through electronic imagery and surveillance?

      Choose one new media technology (CGI, gaming consoles, virtual reality, the Internet, digital, widescreen TV, WebCam, digital camcorders, etc.) and argue for and against the idea that it contributes to the visualisation of culture - that it privileges sight/seeing over all other senses.

1.5

Virtual Reality

❝*...a system which provides a realistic sense of being immersed in an environment. VR is a computer-generated visual, audible and tactile multimedia experience.*❞
(Featherstone and Burrows, 1995, p5-6)

Virtual Reality (VR) is one of the key electronic devices drawn into the debate about the impact of the image on human experience.

VR is a truly interactive computer simulated environment where the user gets to see, feel, hear and move around in a three-dimensional 'virtual' world. Users wear *stereo headphones*, *eyephones* that generate three dimensionality, *datagloves* and *datasuits* that send and receive signals to the computer so that it can programme the environment to match movement and sensation.

In pairs

1.   Devise and design a fantasy-based virtual reality environment. To do this you will need to think of:

   •   *A themed setting* (castle, alien world, haunted house, enchanted forest, underwater city, etc.), that needs to look, sound and feel like it is a real environment for the user.

   •   *Virtual characters* (human and non-human) for the user to interact with.

   •   *Command instructions* for the computer so that it can manipulate the environment as the virtual user moves around it.

You can either produce a *written account* of your virtual world *and/or* you can produce a *series of drawings* to capture this fantasy world.

2.   What problems might arise from people spending a lot of their time in 'virtual reality'? Try to put together a list of 5 dangers that might come from people living in a virtual word.

**The New Media and the Rise of The Information Society I
Information Overload!**

*"Contemporary culture is manifestly more heavily
information laden than any of its predecessors. We exist in
a media-saturated environment."*
(Webster, 1994, p18)

The processing, storage, and transmission of all kinds of information
is a dominant feature of the modern world.

The computer chip, digital satellite and the Internet all allow information
to be processed at ever greater speeds, stored virtually in ever greater
amounts, and transmitted to the most far off places on the planet in a
matter of seconds. Information, as a consequence, is not only everywhere
but also of paramount importance to the way people communicate with
each other, learn about the world, and to the way they conduct business.

Task

In groups of 3 or 4

1. List all the media technologies and media texts that are
    involved in the transmission of information.

    Does it seem that there is too much media generated information
    in the world today? Justify your arguments if you can.

2. For each media technology and media text you have identified
    rate on a scale of 1-10 how accurate and how reliable you
    think the information they provide is. Ask yourself:

    *   Can the media be trusted to present information fairly?

    *   Can you rely on the media to help with homework, or to
        make decisions about holidays, travel, the weather,
        political issues and far-off conflicts?

    *   What evidence or examples do you have to support your
        position on this?

3. If you think you cannot always trust or rely on media generated
    information, where else can you go to find out about the world?

**The New Media and the Rise of The Information Society II
The Poverty of Information**

Access to a great deal of the information generated by the media is actually outside the experiences of a great deal of people living in the world today. Hamelink (1990), found the following differences in *'information access'*:

- 96 per cent of the world's computer hardware is owned by so called first world countries.

- 75 per cent of the world's telephones can be found in the 9 richest countries.

- The poorest countries in the world own less than 10 per cent of telephones.

- Japan has more telephones than in all the countries of Africa.

- In 69 so-called third world countries there were no newspapers or there is only one.

- Europe produces more than 120,000 new books every year, while Africa produces fewer than 350.

- Europe averages 1,400 libraries per country, compared to 18 per country in Africa.

Research Task

In pairs

1. Using the library, the Internet, and CD-ROM try to find out the percentage of people in Britain who own an *Internet-ready Home Computer; digital television; DVD player; games console; mobile phone.*

Using these percentages to help you, answer this two-part question,

2. Is there a technological underclass in Britain - people who do not have direct access to the new media and the information they provide? If so, is there really an abundance of information for everyone in the world today?

The New Media and Postmodernism

Postmodern theory argues that through the new media the way people experience reality has been fundamentally altered. This sense of an 'altered reality' manifests itself in the following ways:

- Through the Internet people can explore their identities (by pretending to be people they are not) in ways which make the notion of 'who am I' open to change.

- People increasingly mix-up, cannot tell the difference between virtual reality and the reality of the 'real' world.

- The world appears to shrink as new media technologies wire the world in instantaneous exchanges.

- People prefer the simulated environment (the holodeck) to the natural environment.

Task

Write a treatment for a new science fiction film where people only experience the world through virtual media devices and new media technologies. Your treatment should include:

a) A *title* for the film.
b) An outline of the *plot* and of the *central characters*.
c) A *storyboard* of the first 12 shots of the film.
d) A *poster* advertising the film.

The Digital Camera

Increasingly digital video (DV) cameras have become the preferred format for shooting both documentary and full length feature films, replacing the hitherto industry standard use of 8mm, Super-8 mm, 16mm, and 32mm film cameras. DV supposedly has a number of advantages over celluloid/reel film cameras:

- The cameras are more mobile and generally lighter to use.

- The cameras are easier to operate.

- The costs of shooting and editing are reduced, particularly because DV cameras do not use film stock, which is more expensive to shoot with and process.

- Shooting 'complex' scenes is easier to organise, especially in relation to the relative ease with which light source can be monitored (unlike the arduous lighting systems needed for shooting on celluloid).

Research Task

In groups of 3 or 4

Using the library and the Internet try to find out:

1. What each of the following film formats are:
   DV, *Super-8mm*, and *32mm*.

2. Why certain filmmakers still prefer to shoot on 32mm film (what does shooting on reel film bring to an image or scene that DV can't?).

Put together an *A4 fact file* of what you find out.

Special Effects

Increasingly almost all fiction films have one or two different types of digital special effect:

- *Invisible special effects* that are not meant to be noticed (as special effects) by film spectators.

- *Visible special effects* which, having produced some wondrous, fantastic, out-of-this-world creation, solicits the 'Wow! That can't be real' reaction from spectators and audiences.

The digitally created dinosaurs in *Jurassic Park* (Spielberg, 1993) and the action-spectacle sequences in *The Matrix* (Wachowski Brothers, 1999) are two recent 'Wow!' examples of visible special effects. However, *Titanic* (Cameron, 1997) is an excellent example of a film that is most remembered for its visible digital special effects, namely in the form of the ship, but which is actually saturated in moments of invisible special effects, whether it be the simulation of Southampton Docks, waves crashing against the vessel, or passengers walking on the decks as the ship sails away into the distance. These are all the work of the special effects department.

Research Task

In groups of 3 or 4

1. Choose one of the films listed below and find out as much as you can about the special effects that were used in the film.

2. Choose two key sequences from this film: one sequence needs to have invisible special effects in it; the other sequence needs to have visible special effects. Show both sequences to the rest of the class and

   a) Get the class to see if they can spot the invisible special effects in the first sequence.

   b) Talk through with the class how the special effects were produced in the second sequence shown.

Gladiator; Blade II; *The Phantom Menace*; Godzilla; *The Mummy Returns*; The Haunting; *Titanic*; Mission Impossible II; *The Matrix*.

2.3

The IMAX Cinema Experience

IMAX combines a horizontally-run 70mm film with screen size as large as 100ft x 75ft. The screen itself is slightly curved and with seating arranged in closer proximity, so that the screen feels like it is almost on top of the audience, consequently putting them in closer touch with the films that are shown. This *sensory experience* is extended through the development of

- Hemispherical screens or *OmnIMAX*;

- *3D IMAX*, in which audiences are required to wear '3D' glasses that render the film image 3-dimensional (3D IMAX films are so designed that missiles, landscapes, animals, etc. appear to touch or rush towards the audience);

- *Showscan*, which combines the large screen format of IMAX with synchronised, moving and tilting seats in the auditorium. Spectators no longer just watch a film, *they live it*, more able than ever before to 'enter' its imaginings.

Task

You have been asked to make a 3D IMAX film about life in the North Pole. This film will capture the rugged but beautiful landscape, the wildlife, the changing seasons, etc. and because the film will be shown in 3D you want the most dramatic footage possible so that audiences feel like they are actually there.

1. Produce a storyboard for the first two minutes of the film.

2. Produce a 500 word description of one scene that particularly exploits the 3D format.

Note: it may be useful to undertake some research on both 3D IMAX and the environment of the North Pole.

The Home Cinema Experience

Increasingly, watching movies at home is very like watching movies at the cinema. With the technological developments in widescreen, digital television, television screen size (66cm) and shape (flatscreen), and digital Surround Sound, the home movie viewing experience has all the spectacle, thrill and scale of the cinema experience.

 **Task**

In pairs

On Trial: The Home Cinema Experience

1. You have been asked to prepare *either*

    A 'prosecution' case that argues the home cinema experience is *inferior* to the cinema experience;

Or

    A 'defence' case that defends and champions the home cinema experience - as an experience that is *superior* to watching a movie at the cinema.

2. Decide between you which role you would like to take - defence or prosecution counsel.

    Then individually put together your case in a form that can be presented in a mock trial.

You want the presentation of your case to last around two minutes.

The rest of the class can be judge and jury, and they can vote on what they think is the most convincing case presented.

2.5

The End of Narrative Cinema?

It can be argued that the increasing use of digital special effects in modern cinema makes it a medium that is over-reliant on spectacle, a medium that is purely a visual, sensory one.

For example, the visual, kinetic delight of visible special effects 'do away with' narrative or plot development, proper characterisation, or dramatic and serious (human) encounter. Ridley Scott's *Gladiator* (2000) is arguably an example of this: it is the digital reconstruction of Rome, the Coliseum, the roaring crowds, the spectacular fight sequences, and ultimately the digital 'reincarnation' of Oliver Reed (who died while making the film) that makes the film a visual rather than a narrative experience.

(Task)

Using the library, the Internet, and CD-ROM to help you, answer this question in a 500 word essay:

Are modern films too dependent on digital special effects? Give reasons and examples for your answer wherever possible.

The End of American Studio Domination?

Digital film-making technology enables young independent film-makers to make films cheaply, with small crews, without the skill levels that are needed for shooting on other formats, such as 'reel' film. Computer mediated communication technologies such as the Internet have provided these new independent digital film-makers with a distribution/transmission space that requires little investment to use, and which circumvent the normal 'public' distribution and exhibition sites for film (which are dominated by the American studios).

A film made on a DV camera can then be edited 'at home', on a sophisticated 'domestic' editing software package, and then 'sold' to Internet distribution companies to stream on-line.

Research Task

Using the library, CD-ROM, and the Internet (especially film-based websites such as the Internet Movie Database):

1. Write up the production history of one film that was shot using digital film technology (this could range from computer generated films such as *Ice Age* [2002], to small budget DV films such as *Time Code* [2000])

2. Try to visit an Internet based film company (such as *iBeam* and *CinemaNow*) and learn as much as you can about the way they work. Again, write up your notes, putting them together in an *A4 fact file*.

3. In your opinion, is it a good or bad thing that digital film-making has the potential to lessen the control that American film studios have over the film industry? Give reasons for your answer.

The Death of Cinema...?

One can argue that in the digital age, reel (celluloid) film-making is in astate of terminal decline and will very quickly die out. The argument runs that because digital is cheaper, because the image that it produces is more robust and yet more flexible, and because it is easier to use, film-makers will abandon celluloid altogether in the digital age.

Also, with the potential digitalisation of cinemas, and the increasing use of the Internet to stream videos, the theatres where reel film can be shown are likely to diminish in numbers until they become mere museum pieces. Just as today preservation groups place into heritage old 'Picture Palaces', tomorrow they will put preservation orders on projection rooms where celluloid was once put on flatbed 'platters'.

(Task)

"Technologically, film - at least as theatrically exhibited - is very antiquated. We still show moving pictures the way the Lumières did, pumping electric light through semi-transparent cells, projecting shadows on a white screen. These techniques belong in a museum. A change is overdue."
(Paul Schrader, 1996, p204)

1. Read the above quotation from the screenwriter/film-maker Paul Schrader.

    Do you agree with him that the way films are currently exhibited (projected) are outdated and should now 'belong in a museum'?

    What criticisms could you make of Schrader's position - what counter-arguments can you come up with to defend the way films are currently exhibited? (It might be helpful here to refer to the work you did in exercise 2.1, research task 2.)

2. Class discussion:

    Project yourself ten years into the future. What will cinemas be like? Will there be projection rooms and projectionists showing 35mm film? Or will digital be the dominant technology? Will virtual reality and IMAX be the main ways that people experience fictional films?

A History of Change

Television has always been a medium/media caught up in the processes of (technological) transformation. If one was to look at the origins of television in this country one would find a remarkably different broadcasting climate from the one that exists today.

Only 400 black and white sets, operating in London, were available to receive the BBC's inaugural service from Alexandra Palace in November 1936. A TV set cost £100 or more - roughly the same price then as a new car – and was therefore considered to be a luxury item. There was only one station broadcast, with a limited range of programming, on for a few hours a day. There were no adverts on TV in 1936, and an outside (terrestrial) arial was all that was needed to receive this one channel.

Task

1. Using the above description of what TV was like in the UK in 1936, produce a list of all the changes that have since taken place.

2. Using the heading 'Television Today' produce an *A4 fact file* of what the modern television landscape is like.

   Here is a list of things that you might want to consider when answering these questions:

   number of channels; colour; adverts; *the remote control*; High Definition Television (HDTV); *digital Surround Sound*; Plasma screens; *widescreen*; fastext; *video, DVD, and game playing*; digital satellite television; *digital terrestrial television*; and multimedia interactivity.

3.2

Digital Nirvana - background

It can be argued that the development of digital satellite television (DST) has had the following major benefits for viewers:

- Digital TV has increased viewer choice to over 200 channels, many available 24 hours a day, and many of which are dedicated 'niche' services offering everything from religious programming, science and wildlife documentaries, to arts, music and sports programmes. In the digital age almost everything is available to view - including pornography - if the viewer wants it.

- Digital TV has heralded the age of the multimedia environment, where television becomes a multi-use media station. Digital TV is used for movie watching, game playing, video recording, emailing and shopping.

- Digital TV has heralded an age of full viewer interactivity. With digital technology viewers can choose their own movies to watch, shop for clothes, book music and theatre tickets, email friends, check their bank accounts, record 'live TV' and, in terms of sports programmes, can choose their own camera angles to watch the game.

- Digital TV opens up the TV environment to global influences and experiences. With over 200 channels viewers have access to TV stations/programmes from around the globe (including India and the Middle East). Digital TV is therefore part of the process where increasingly the world is experienced as a 'global village', with different cultures meeting and greeting one another.

- Digital TV transforms the presentation of TV and the content of TV programmes. The new screen technologies produce a better TV image, with higher definition and improved colour; a bigger, flatter screen size; and digital Surround Sound that can fill a room. The new CGI technologies allow special effects to shape any number of TV genres in new and imaginative ways.

Digital Nirvana

Research Task

- -

1. Choose two of the channels listed below and find out as much
    as you can about what they broadcast, when they broadcast,
    who owns the channel, and whether a subscription fee has to
    be paid to view. Put the information you find into an *A4 fact file*.

    The History Channel   *Discovery*
    Animal Planet   National Geographic
    MTV   *The Sci-Fi Channel*
    Sky Sports   TCM
    Artsworld   *B4U*
    Sky MovieMax   Lifestyle TV

2. Undertake a seven-day survey of how the (main) TV is used in
    your home. You might want to establish the following: times of
    the day it is in use; name of user; the use that the TV is being
    put to at that time; and the length of time spent at on that use
    at any one time. For example:

Day	Time	User	TV use
Monday	7.30-8.00 am	Brother	PlayStation
	8.00-8.30	Me/Brother	cartoons
	9.30-10.30	Dad	video recording

Try to present your results statistically (pie charts, graphs, tables,
etc.) but also with an explanation of what you think you have found
out.

3.4

Digital Nirvana II - What A Goal! Football on Sky

With the development of Sky's digital (satellite) presentation of Premiership football, TV sport became truly interactive.

Viewers of Premiership football have the ability to choose their own camera angles with which to watch the game; they can track a particular players movement on 'PlayerCam'; they can watch the highlights so far while the 'live' game is still being played; and they can choose to listen to partisan commentary from their own supporters. This type of interactivity, combined with the use of on-screen hi-tech graphics and mobile cameras on the touchline, enriches the experience of watching televised sport. For the football fan (who can afford to pay) digital nirvana indeed.

In groups of 3 or 4

You have been asked to produce a hi-tech, 'interactive' digital TV programme for one of the sports listed below. The commissioners want you to detail how you will make the coverage more exciting, and what interactive features there will be. They want this to be the most fully interactive sports programme ever. Choose one of these sports (events):

Tennis (Wimbledon)	*Motor Racing*	Golf	*Cricket*
Gymnastics	Athletics	*Darts*	Snooker

1. You will need to come up with a four page 'pitch' that details the exciting elements you are proposing. The pitch should be a mixture of description/rationale, and diagrams/simulations of what the programme will look like (including its interactive features).

    Try to think not only about the style of the coverage during the game, but also about its format in the studio before, after, and during any organised breaks in the game.

2. Present your 'pitch' to the rest of the class, giving your group 5 to 10 minutes to present its proposals.

Digital Hell

There are a number of criticisms that can be made about the digital television revolution:

- Digital TV doesn't actually create greater viewer choice but only the illusion of choice since most channels are full of the same types of programmes. Consequently, innovative programming and programmes for minority groups get erased in the new dawn of the digital age.

- If one cannot afford to pay the subscription or pay-per-view fees for access to digital TV then one is left off the broadcasting map - one becomes a member of the technological underclass. These people then actually have even *less choice* than before, especially in relation to the major sporting events that used to be free-to-air on terrestrial television.

- The interactivity at the core of the digital TV experience is relatively mindless and escapist. As it stands it largely consists of game playing, shopping, and, for football fans, accruing statistics and figures, and following their favourite players on-screen. Interactivity, as it is presently experienced, actually takes TV further away from the idea that it should add to the democratic process by providing a public forum for discussing the most important issues of the day.

- Finally, digital TV does not really provide the opportunity for people to experience cultures from across the globe but rather offers them the chance to 'shop' for these experiences, turning the global village into one great shopping centre.

Essay question:

Digital TV has done more harm than good to the way television is experienced in the UK. Discuss this statement, using examples wherever you can, in about 500 words.

3.6

Digital Hell II – Television News

The argument that Digital TV produces programmes that are much more visual, interactive and exciting is contested by the argument which suggests that what it actually does is empty programmes of their 'content', of their concern for/with narrative development, or for/with serious issues.

In this counter-argument what Digital TV does is make the image, the spectacle and the special effect reign supreme so that TV loses its ability to address and report on the most complex of political and cultural issues of the day. The digitalisation of television news is an excellent case study for looking at this emptying out of content.

Task

Choose one national news bulletin and analyse it according to the argument that it is more concerned with spectacle, action, and the dramatic than it is with serious, detailed reporting.

- Look out for any graphics, simulations, or special effects that are used in the bulletin - either to capture a story or to add to the way the story is being imagined.

- Look out for 'live' reports (hand-held camera work, the reporter being caught up in the midst of the action).

- Try to find out about how the title sequence and studio space was constructed. How important was visual appeal to this?

> *Virtually all forms of music-making are dependent upon some kind of deliberately designed and specialised equipment or technology...The history of musical instruments is always, in this sense, a history of technology.*
> **(Durant, 1994, p178)**

Research Task

1. Choose one of the musical instruments listed below and find out how and what technologies were involved in its origins and in its development as a musical instrument.

   The Guitar

   The Piano

   The Synthesiser

   The Drums

2. *Produce an A4 fact file* of the history of your chosen musical instrument.

4.2

Recording Popular Music in the Digital Studio

"A musician/artist is now often producer, performer and engineer too... A new species of digital auteur exists, who is able to compose and produce music on a single computer and even create a CD of their work at the end of the process."
(Gilbert and Pearson, 1999, p118)

The recording of popular music today is so bound up with technological processes that a musical track can be produced in the recording studio without the use of musicians or singers. A producer can lay a track from start to finish, with instruments, riffs, drum beats, samples, melodies and vocals all called up from a resource databank, digital sampler, and then mixed or 'engineered' on a PC with a software package such as Avid's Pro Tools.

Research Task

1. Using the library, the Internet and CD-ROM to help you, try to find out how the following digital processes have transformed the way popular music is recorded in the studio:

The (digital) synthesiser	*The digital sampler*
The drum machine	Digital computer sequencers
Comping	*MIDI (musical instrument digital interface)*

2. Do you think that digital technology has begun to eliminate the need for real musicians and real instrumentation to be involved in the studio recording process?

    Is this a dangerous development? Discuss your ideas with the rest of the class.

Electronic Dance Music

" In industrial and techno music ... groups such as Frontline Assembly, Front 242, *and* KMFDM *create a wall of noise, using explosive beats, broad-band synthesiser pulses, and fragmentary spoken-word samples; they mimic and (to some) satirise the empty plenitude and disconnected tones of post-industrial life. "*

(Potter, 1998, p40)

Dance music, which first emerged in the UK during the early 1980s, is made up of a range of different musical styles or sub-genres; Acid House; (Chicago) House; (Detroit) Techno; Euro-House; Jungle/ Drum 'n' Bass; Hardcore; Industrial; Hip-Hop, etc. What all these sub-genres have in common is the *electronic production of sound -* musical composition and performance that relies on and utilises synthesisers, drum machines, samplers, and sequencers. Dance music is a (digital) electronic mode of production with a number of 'programmed' recurring musical features, generated by computers, and performed in dance clubs to clubbers who immerse themselves in what is pulsating wall of noise.

In groups of 3 or 4

1. Choose one of the dance music sub-genres mentioned in the list above, and produce an account of how it works musically, of the pleasures it offers the people who listen and dance to it.

2. Choose one dance track that you are familiar with and that you like. Bring the track to the class to play, with an explanation of why you think this track is so successful.

3. If you were able to record a dance track in a studio what things would you be looking to include. What would your soundscape be like? Put together a track outline.

4. Why do you think people go to clubs to dance? Is it an escapist experience - a chance to free oneself from the routines of everyday life? Share your ideas with the rest of the class.

4.4

Popular Music in the Multimedia Home

Popular music can be listened to and watched in the home on a range of devices including the mini-disc player; the midi hi-fi system; the personal stereo; the multimedia PC with CD-ROM, CD-R and DVD; the Internet (where music can be downloaded, saved and burnt onto CD); the digital television, in the form of music shows such as *Top of the Pops*, and TV music stations such as MTV and VH1; the video and DVD player that plays music video compilations; and radio and digital radio that transmits 24 hours a day, 7 days a week.

New media technologies have so enabled the listening and watching of popular music that it can be listened to communally, in any room in the house, or privately, in the bedroom, through headphones or the personal stereo, and it can be watched collectively or privately on the television and on the PC. In short, new media technologies have massively opened up the ability for popular music to penetrate the home environment.

(Task)

1. List all the electronic devices that enable music to be played in the home. Divide the list up into the areas of the home where these electrical devices can be found; for example, under 'in the bedroom' you would list the radio alarm clock, the personal stereo, etc.

    *   Which room has the most electronic devices to play music?

    *   Which room has the least?

    *   Is there any room where music cannot be listened to? If so, why this room?

2. Think about how music is listened to in the home. Has *listening* to music actually become more *visual*? List all the different ways that music is now visualised or given a visual representation in the home.

Popular Music in the Multimedia Home II
MTV

MTV, launched in America in 1981, is a 24-hour music video station available on cable, satellite and digital TV. The music videos shown on MTV are renowned for their rapid edits, dizzying camera work, glossy visuals, special effects and high quota of sex and violence. Music videos shown on MTV help promote single and album sales, tours and the artist's back catalogue.

It is argued that MTV changes the very nature of how music is produced and consumed because artists and record companies increasingly rely on (MTV playing) the music video to reach new and diverse audiences around the world. Great expense is put into producing a video that positions the artist in a favourable light - they are styled and imaged in a way that makes them sexual or potent or heroic visual stars. Similarly, audiences increasingly rely on the music video and the 'look' of the artist to influence their record buying.

 **Task**

In groups of 3 or 4

A major record company has asked you to produce a music video for one of their new heavy metal/grunge artists, Liquid Metal. To help you do this you have been given a design brief to follow. The brief asks you to create a raw, uncompromising image for the four-member, all male band. The single the video accompanies is called *Broken Stones*, a song about teenage alienation. The record company wants the video to be able to be aired at any time on MTV 2, the 'alternative' music television channel, so there are censorship issues to consider. You have a large budget for this, so location shooting in the US, or anywhere in the world, is not a problem.

1. Come up with a two-page outline of what you want in the video - its themes, structure, setting, and overall narrative.

2. Produce a full storyboard for the video - one that includes an indication of shot length, camera angle and position, *mise-en-scène*, and the types of edit that move you from shot to shot.

4.6

Do-It-Yourself-Digital-Music

Much of the digital hardware and software that has transformed the recording studio is also available in the high street at a relatively low cost. Drum machines, synthesisers, sequencers and samplers, DAT machines and MIDI can all be bought at the local electric store and assembled or connected up in the home for 'digital auteurs' to multi-task their own musical tracks. Through the Internet these digital auteurs can also download samples, riffs, vocals, sound effects, etc. from a variety of sources to layer their electronic songs in ever more complex and innovative ways.

Similarly, for rock and pop bands that play real instruments, the garage or the loft can become the studio setting, with digital recording equipment capturing the performances. These individual tracks or whole albums can then be run off in CD form and sold at gigs or sent on to A&R people at the major record companies or they can be distributed on the Net, either through the band's/artist's own Web page, or independent music providers, or on to radio stations and record companies that have online portals.

Task

1. Reading through the above summary of how digital technology and the Internet have transformed the way music can be recorded, describe in your own words the processes that one would go through to record a single track at home.

   - What are the advantages of producing music at home in this way?

   - What are the *disadvantages* of producing music at home in this way?

2. Choose one of the artists named below and do some research on how they used home recording equipment to lay their first tracks.

   Gomez
   Brian Eno
   Cornershop
   Aphex Twin

The Home Computer

The multimedia, Internet-ready home computer has transformed the way people work, take part in leisure and entertainment activities, educate and inform themselves about the world, and the way finance and commercial activities can be undertaken. A list of the functions of the multimedia home PC would show that it is used for:

- *Game playing*
- Home movie watching and the streaming of movies 'online'
- *Watching television*
- Listening to music
- *Watching music videos or 'live' shows*
- Downloading music, or for copying music on CD-R
- *Watching and downloading pornography*
- Information finding and gathering and information application
- *Word processing (letters, reports, CVs, business documents, etc.)*
- Desktop publishing
- *Producing digital/virtual photo albums*
- Film and video editing
- *Music composition and recording, and virtual distribution*
- Communication
- *Shopping and browsing*
- Checking personal financial details and for paying bills online
- *Political activities*
- Criminal activities

Task

1. Using the list above, rank in ascending order the uses that you think the home computer is most put to (numbers should run from **1 = most use - to 18 = least use**). Try to explain your decisions to the rest of the class

2. How central do you think the home computer is to everyday life? Imagine a world without home computers (or computers generally) What would it be like? Describe this world in approximately 250 words.

5.2

The Internet

The origins of the Internet lie in a US Department of Defense sponsored research project, Arpanet, in the late 1960s. Arpanet was designed to link computers across the US to enable military scientists to share their resources or computer data.

However, the commercial and public-wide development of the Internet - the Internet as we know it today - didn't really begin until the early to mid 1990s with the establishment of the *World Wide Web* ('the Web'), browser software, and the growth in the number of *Internet service providers* (ISPs). These three key developments all played a major role in the expansion of the mass use of the Net as the dominant media/medium that people go to for information, consumption and entertainment.

Research Task

- -

In pairs and using the library, the Internet, and CD-ROM:

1. Research the full history and the development of the Internet from its beginnings in the late 1960s. How different is the Internet today from these early beginnings? Put together a 'then' and 'now' contrast sheet and share this information with the rest of the class.

2. Define the following key Internet terms

World Wide Web	*Internet service provider*
browser software	Cookies
email	*chatroom*
search engines	

3. What benefits has the Internet brought to people? Put together a list of what you collectively feel are the most important benefits.

4. Is there a downside to the Internet? What problems does electronic communication throw up? Share your ideas with the rest of the class.

Virtual Communities

"People in virtual communities use words on screens to exchange pleasantries and argue, engage in intellectual discourse, conduct commerce, exchange knowledge… gossip, feud, fall in love, find friends and lose them, play games, flirt, create a little high art and a lot of idle talk. People in virtual communities do just about everything people do in real life, but we leave our bodies behind."
(Rheingold, 1999, p275)

A virtual community evolves from bulletin-board systems (known as BBSs), where members of the community leave and retrieve messages, photographs, digital images; 'publish' reviews, statements, arguments; ascribe and demarcate roles for members of the community; and agree common aims and objectives (for those communities that are goal orientated). In terms of what communities exist online one finds BBSs on everything from cult books, films and music, to sexual preferences, religion, and a whole plethora of hobbies and interests.

Task

In groups of 3 or 4

1. You have decided to start up a virtual community for one of the following areas of shared interest:

    UK Dance Music   *Hong Kong Action Film*
    Ice Hockey   Youth Against Poverty   *Save Our Forests*

    - Decide how you want the bulletin boards to be used - what are your aims and objectives for this virtual community?

    - Devise a list of aims and objectives for the BBS.

    - Produce a number of 'messages' that you would expect to be passed between members.

    - Put together a profile of the type of people who would use this particular BBS.

2. Are virtual communities 'real' communities? Do they have the same sort of supportive networks and ties as the communities we physically live in day-to-day? If not, why not?

Multi-User Domains

Multi-User Domains (MUDs) are online, networked, text-based computer programmes that allow participants to interact with each other in virtual, often fantasy-based environments. The MUD interface is a window or portal into another world, where game players take on roles that they script and construct for themselves.

All the role playing, interaction and scene setting that takes place in MUDs are done through words or text-based messages. Such interaction is generally carried out through a universally applied command structure involving commands such as *say*, *emote*, *whisper*, and *page*. These commands allow users to speak to one another openly (*say* command); express emotive sentiments to other users (*emote* command), speak secretly or privately to particular users in a multi-user context (*whisper* command), and to speak to another user who may be in a different virtual setting (*page* command). The keyboard is vital to the complexity of the communication that can take place. Through the use of *'emoticons'* (understood by tilting your head to the left) role playing can also become pictorial:

:)	becomes a smiling face
;)	becomes a winking, smiling face
8-)	becomes someone wearing glasses
<:-o	becomes someone screaming in fright, with his or her hair standing on end
:-&	becomes someone who will keep a secret

In pairs (you will need shared access to a PC for this exercise)

1. Try to communicate with one another using the command structure and the emoticons outlined above - if you can think of other emoticons then add them to your list.

    How difficult is it to communicate like this? Is it boring? Why?

2. Now imagine that you are both prisoners in a wet, cold, rat-infested jail with guards trying to listen to you communicate. Electronically *whisper* to one another about how you intend to escape. Is this more enjoyable? Why?

The Internet and the Global Revolution

The Internet is one of the key new media involved in opening up the world to mediated communication. People can email one another from the four corners of the planet, attaching photographs, video clips, birthday cards, business reports and all manner of business documentation. Travellers to distant places can keep in touch with loved ones at home, and people who cannot afford to travel can get the travel experience - multimedia knowledge of the world - by sitting in front of their computers and browsing holiday, government and commercial based Web sites for this information. The Internet, then, is the one new media technology that literally makes the world feel like it is a smaller place, a 'global village' **(McLuhan, 1989)**.

Research Task

Internet Travelling

1. Using the Internet try to find out about the geography, climate and cultures of 5 countries that you have never been to. Print this information and in your own words put together a description of each country.

    Use your school/college's ISP homepage and search engine to help you.

2. What is Internet travelling like? Is it as good as the real thing? If not, what doesn't virtual travel have that real travel does? Share your ideas with the rest of the class.

5.6

The Internet and the Shopping Experience

It can be argued that the whole Internet experience is nothing more than a shopping experience. To go online one has to have an *account* with an Internet service provider (ISP) - calls are metered and *charged* along with normal telephone calls, or else a flat monthly *fee* is paid to the ISP for the Internet call chargers made that month. Once online, the user is bombarded with electronic *adverts*, *flyers*, and *pop-ups selling* everything from loans, mortgages, CDs, holidays, cars, games, insurance, DVDs, flowers, wines, books, etc.

The homepage that the user arrives at is actually one gigantic interactive advert made up of multiple advertising texts that if 'clicked' on are portals to other commercial sites, and other interactive adverts, in what becomes a never ending trail of selling. One can click on an advert for a bookstore, and three or four pop-ups will appear in succession selling you something else, taking you to another commercial site.

This consumption experience is extended into the virtual shopping worlds that one can enter into. Virtual worlds with shopping aisles, departments, bargain and offer areas and till machines. In these virtual shops users can see the goods, which are sold through the same sort of value transference found in normal advertising (exotic locations, beautiful models, etc.).

In pairs

1. Devise and design a series of online adverts for a new brand of aftershave. These adverts need to employ the interactive nature of the Internet and the audio-visual aspects of this electronic media.

    • Produce 3 sketches of your ideas for these adverts, or, if you have the software at your school/college, 3 virtual adverts.

    • Present these adverts to the rest of the class, with explanations of how they would work, and why.

2. Do you agree with the arguments outlined above? Go back to them and offer 3 criticisms of the observations that are made?

The Gaming Revolution in the Home

In the modern home, there are numerous electronic devices that involve or allow game playing to take place; on the home computer, in CD or DVD format; online in MUDs or game orientated Web sites, or from software downloaded onto the hard drive of the computer; on interactive digital TV (through game playing menu options); on gaming consoles plugged into the TV (such as PlayStation (2), Xbox, and Gamecube); on hand-held gaming consoles (such as Game Boy Color and Game Boy Advance); and on communication or telecommunication devices such as calculators, watches and mobile phones. In this gaming revolution of the home, the whole family, in different rooms, on different hardware, with different software, can all be game playing simultaneously.

Research Task

You want to find out how much game playing goes on in your home. Ask each member of your family the following questions:

1. What electronic games do you play at home?

2. How often do you play these electronic games (where, when and for how long do you play)?

3. Why do you play these games at home? What pleasures do you get from playing these electronic games (escapism, competition, relaxation, boredom)?

Put your results together in a table or chart and then explain your results. Think about whether gender, age and role affect the responses that family members give. Do your parents respond differently, for example?

Family member	Electronic game	Where	When	Length	Why

6.2

The Gaming Revolution and the Film Industry

Much of the digital and CGI technology that has gone into transforming film production, and the 'spectacle' appeal of modern film, find their way into the technology that drives the gaming console and the visual appeal of the games. The kinetic, visceral, special effect-laden modern film finds its equivalent in the fast paced, high-octane action, fantasy and science fiction-based narratives of the interactive electronic game.

But not only this, successful console games such as *Tomb Raider, Pokemon, Final Fantasy* are re-made as Hollywood blockbuster films, and similarly, successful Hollywood film franchises, such as James Bond or *Star Wars (1977)*, find their way into and are re-imagined for the games console. With technical advances in television sound and picture quality, game playing in the home takes on the 'scale' of film watching in the cinema.

In groups of 3 or 4

1. You have been asked to develop one of the following Hollywood films into an electronic game for playing on one of the leading consoles: *Spy Kids 2, Minority Report, Rush Hour 2, Dr. Dolittle*. There is a large budget for this.

   The first thing you will need to do is research the different genres and gaming formats so that you have a real sense of how games work.

2. Your development work will need to include the following items:

   * A description of your 'concept' for the game - its structure, levels of interactivity, pleasures it offers, and its links to the movie it is based on.
   * A design cover for its CD (DVD) case to include its title, graphics, and supporting text.
   * Sketches and descriptions of three or four of the main characters.

3. Present or 'pitch' your ideas to the rest of the class.

The Gaming Revolution and Anti-social Behaviour - background

It has been argued that people who spend a lot of their time console game playing develop anti-social characteristics. It is suggested that console game playing does this because:

• Game playing is harmfully *addictive*. The compulsion elements of the game force the player to return again and again to the console at the point where they left off. The addiction feeds into wanting more games, and more time to play the games.

• Game playing produces *disinhibition*, *imitation* and *desensitisation* effects. Game players adopt or copy out the violence and the sexualised encounters found in the fantasy game environment in the real world. At the same time the level and graphic nature of the violence needed to produce the thrill effect has to be continually increased.

• Game playing (often) involves *sexist*, *racist*, and *homophobic role models* and stereotyping. Female action characters are sexualised, or else are sex role stereotyped (victims, virgins, damsels in distress) who need protecting. Villains are often given ethnic (Oriental, South American, African) names and physical characteristics, or else are disfigured or symbolically coded as homosexual (camp, feminine).

• The competition and individualism at the core of game playing helps produce *selfish*, *driven individuals* who favour competition and individualism above community values and group solidarity.

• Continuous immersion in the game playing environment produces players with *short concentration spans*. The visual fix of the game, the rapid, fast moving nature of the encounters, and the structure of games which split interaction into levels, time zones, and races (players have to repeatedly go against the clock) produces players who can only recall in bite size chunks, who can only pay attention for 'gaming minutes'.

6.4

The Gaming Revolution and Anti-social Behaviour

Research Task

In groups of 3 or 4

To complete this task you will need access to a games console and at least 3 or 4 games.

1. Arrange for the group to meet at a venue/home where you have been given permission to use a games console for 2-3 hours.

   • Choose 3 (2-player mode) games to play and take it in turns to play one another as well as the computer.

   • Take individual notes before and after the game about the way you are feeling (adrenaline rush, competitive, angry, elated, etc.) and on whether you think the game is addictive, too violent, and sexist/racist. Try not to share your notes with the other game players until your next lesson.

2. For the last 30 minutes of your gaming session turn your collective attention to analysing the structure, themes, goals and characters of one of the games you have been playing - and apply the anti-social criteria outlined above to it.

3. Put together *an A4 profile* of the game you looked at in depth and share this, along with your individual notes, with the rest of the class.

Essay Task

How far do you agree with the statement that console game playing produces anti-social behaviour? Use the research you carried out above to help answer this question.

Under Surveillance

One could argue that in the modern world today people are under almost constant surveillance. Whether at home or at work, shopping or clubbing, driving or travelling by public transport people are being filmed, are having information about them stored without their knowledge, and are contactable by phone, fax, email, bleeper, pager, *twentyfourseven*. At the forefront of this surveillance revolution are new media technologies, and in particular the lightweight, mobile digital camera; the (multi-media) mobile phone; and the Internet-ready home PC. Through these electronic devices the distinction between the private and the public, the secret and the visible are eroded, and the control that one has over personal information is lost.

Class discussion:

Is the modern world we live in under surveillance?

To hold this discussion successfully a member of the class will need to act as chair. The chair will organise who speaks and for how long, and will try to involve all members of the class in the discussion.

Class members need to be given 15 minutes to think through the question, and to take up a position.

The discussion should last for 30 minutes, and at the end of the discussion the chair should try to summarise the main points, and whether any conclusions can be usefully drawn.

Big Brother is Watching You

Developments in technology over the last 10 years has transformed the ease with which real events can be filmed and edited by people with very little training and experience. TV producers and programme schedulers have been quick to capitalise on this in a number of ways:

- People's home produced video material can be recycled and used as the primary source for prime time television 'reality' shows such as *You've Been Framed!*

- Documentary film-making increasingly uses either the *video diary format*, where ordinary people can video, narrate and edit their often extraordinary lives for TV viewing, or the *docu-soaps format* - character and crises led documentaries on everything from airports, driving schools and traffic wardens.

- Channel 4's *Big Brother*, a hybrid reality TV show, combines elements of the docu-soap and the game show. Volunteers/contestants are locked up in secure house and put under 24-hour video surveillance. One by one the volunteers are voted off by audiences based on the way they have been perceived through the footage broadcast on TV (and, increasingly, the Web).

- TV news teams and crime shows, such as *Crimewatch*, increasingly rely on amateur video footage to supply the visuals to a story or a criminal investigation. The most powerful recent example of this was the terrorist attack on America on September 11th 2001, where amateur footage captured each of the aeroplanes smashing into their targets.

In pairs

Choose one of the reality TV formats named above (video diary, docu-soap; reality TV; reality/quiz show) and come up with a new idea for a programme.

You will need to come up with a name for the programme; a 250 word description of how it will be structured; a rationale/justification for why it will work, and why audiences will want to watch it.

The Surveillance Revolution and the Surveillance Camera

The use of the digital video camera to record the movement and behaviour of people extends far into everyday life, so much so that it can be argued that we are living in/under a *surveillance culture*.

Today, in shopping centres, high streets, parks, alleyways, roads and schools - in fact, in any public space that has been deemed to be unsafe, or which could be vandalised, or where laws could be broken - the 24-hour surveillance camera is in operation. Generally perched on steel posts 5-10 metres above ground, on moveable heads, the surveillance camera silently surveys the activities of the people who are using the space below. A romantic kiss, a walk in the park, a cycle ride, are indistinguishable to this all-seeing eye from acts of vandalism, assault and drug-taking.

Task

In pairs

1. Think of one space in your hometown that is under surveillance. Describe how this space is surveyed, and put together a list of the reasons for why you think this particular area has been put under surveillance.

2. How does seeing or knowing a surveillance camera is operating in a particular area make you feel (safe, threatened, vulnerable, etc.)? Do you think young people respond differently than 'older' people do to surveillance cameras? Why might there be a difference here?

3. What are the problems or issues raised by surveillance culture? For example, what happens to privacy or freedom of movement in a world where everyone is under some form of surveillance?

4. Finally, having worked through the questions above, do you think there should be this degree of surveillance, or for that matter, any surveillance at all? *Give reasons for your answer*.

7.4

The Surveillance Revolution and The Mobile Phone

The development of the first mobile phones transformed the nature of one-to-one communication, breaking down the private/public divide by making all areas of social life open to communication. No matter where one was - on a train, shopping, out walking, or eating a meal - one could be contacted and one could also contact someone else who had a mobile phone. Important messages, life saving phone calls and business deals could all be made no matter where the person was - a revolution was clearly in the making. In fact one could argue that, like the all-seeing surveillance camera, the all-hearing mobile phone made the social world feel like it could only be experienced as an entirely public domain.

The incorporation of the mobile phone into the language of fashion opened up its potential as a consumption device, drawing it into the world of media production and technical innovation. The mobile phone became *the* symbol of street cred, with the size of the phone (the smaller the better), the ring tones one had (the more the merrier), and the type of facia(s) one had (from mock leopard skin to *Buffy the Vampire Slayer*), being key signifiers of how stylish the user was. With developments in telecommunications the mobile phone became a mobile multi-media station, with WAP (Internet) capabilities and gaming and music functions.

Task

1. How has the multimedia mobile phone changed the nature of everyday life? How are mobile phones used (are they just a fashion accessory - worn to be seen)? What different uses are they put to? How central are they now to the way people communicate?
   Put together a critical review of the modern multi-media mobile phone.

2. Do you agree with the argument that mobile phones contribute to the surveillance culture? Explain and justify your response to this question.

3. If there was an Act of Parliament to ban all mobile phones from public spaces, and you were given a chance to vote, which way would you vote, and why?

The Surveillance Revolution and the Internet

It can be argued that the Internet is involved in the modern world becoming increasingly under surveillance. By using the Internet, by simply connecting a computer to an ISP, the user is opening up their private lives to public scrutiny. Put simply, the user's Internet footprints are always subject to non-detectable surveillance mechanisms. According to David Lyon (1998) these mechanisms manifest in the following ways:

- 'People finding' tools such as Alta Vista gather personal data about people from the user groups they are part of. This information is passed on to commercial companies looking to sell virtual products/services to users.
- Many Web sites automatically create visitors' registers, *'collecting directly from the user's computer data such as the kind of computer you own, your email address and the previous page you visited'* (p92).
- Many Web sites record how the site is being used by a user; habits, purchases made, length of time at the site, and what was viewed there, are collected and passed onto the owners of the Web site.
- 'Data mining' (gathering data about how users us a variety of Web sites) allows commercial companies to predict how, for example, a new Web site or product will be used with different types of users/consumers.
- 'Cookies' (Client-Side Persistent Information) is a central tracking agent that allows Web sites to store information about how, when and which sites have been visited on the hard drive of the user's computer, to be picked up whenever the user return to that/those Web sites.

Research Task

In groups of 3 or 4

1. Try to find out as much information as you can about how the Internet tracks, stores and uses information about people who 'log on'. Put this information into an *A4 file*.

2. Do you think there should be measures (technologies) to stop such surveillance happening? What do you think can or should be done?

8.1

Conclusion - The New (Old) Media and the Modern World

The new media have had a profound effect on the modern media landscape, and on everyday life. They have altered forever the form, content, and reception/consumption of 'old' media such as film, television, and music: and through the home computer, the Internet, the gaming console, and the multimedia mobile phone they have transformed the way people entertain themselves at home, and in public. Digital technology and telecommunications have been the primary motors of what has often been referred to as a revolution. New times indeed, but new times one could argue that we are in the middle of, rather than at the end, with clear, simple conclusions to be drawn. The new media have the potential to offer so much to people's experience of the modern world, but they also have the potential to do much damage.

Task

Drawing together all the ideas, arguments and examples generated through your work on the new media, offer a summarising, concluding view on whether you think the new media bring a greater range of benefits to modern life or whether they bring real dangers to our lives, our cultures, perhaps even the very essences of our humanity. Share your thoughts with the rest of the class.

Task

It is the year 2030 and you have been asked to write an article for a video magazine on the changes that have taken place in the media over the preceding 30 years (from the year 2000 onwards).

Produce this video magazine article (in paper, mock-up form) and look into the future of the new media...

Glossary of Key Terms

Browsers	computer software that enables individuals to search for information on the World Wide Web
Cookies (Client-Side Persistent Information)	a central tracking agent that allows Web sites to store information about how, when and which Web sites have been visited, on the hard drive of the user's computer, to be picked up whenever the user returns to that/those Web sites
Comping	enables the best parts from several takes of a music performance to be seamlessly edited together for the final 'perfect' version. Recording, consequently, is composite rather than singular (one continuous take) in form
Computer Generated Imagery (CGI)	involves using computers to create large-scale action, historical and futuristic scenes for film and television programmes. Such is the growth in CGI that it constitutes a major division of the filmmaking industry, headed by George Lucas' Industrial Light and Magic company. It is also now of course, thanks to Pixar, a developing animated film form. The ground-breaking *Toy Story* (1995) was the first ever complete CGI movie and one that established the trend continued most recently with *Ice Age* (2002)
Computer sequencers	function, in one sense, like a multi-track recorder: *'it records music in an abstract form, as sequences of electronic commands which then must be assigned to voices produced by other machines'* (Toynbee, 2000, p94). Digital sequencers enable short musical 'events' to be programmed and then extended into longer sections, increasing the complexity or the intensity of the available or achievable tempos and rhythms of a track
The Culture of Sight	suggests that we live in an image-based world where seeing is privileged above all other senses. The new media are considered to be above all else seeing technologies
Dance music	is a (digital) electronic mode of production with a number of 'programmed' recurring musical features, with drum patterns, bass lines, lyrics repeated and re-cycled across the length of a track. Dance music relies on and utilises synthesisers, drum machines, samplers, and sequencers
Data mining	or gathering data about how users use a variety of Web sites allows commercial companies to predict how, for example, a new Web site or product will be used by different types of users/consumers
Digital Camera (DV)	meant to be a superior way of reproducing the moving image because, unlike film cameras that use celluloid to record: they do not need lighting systems to be in place; they are more mobile; generally lighter to use; and they reduce the costs of shooting and editing, particularly because they do not use the comparatively more expensive film stock, or need their video formats processing in the same way
Digital broadcast satellite (DBS)	enables a TV set to receive a signal directly from an orbiting satellite, allowing a greater number of channels to be watched at home
Digital satellite television (DST)	introduced by Sky in 1998 with a 200 channel service, Internet and full interactivity capability promised within two years. DST now enables people to make viewing choices, shop, email, and play games – all through a remote control device – making the television a multimedia station

Digital samplers	replicate the exact sounds made by a musician – whether this be in the form of the guitar, cello, saxophone, trumpet, etc. – so that real musicians are no longer needed for the recording process since the sampler can produce these sounds on demand
Digital terrestrial television (DTT)	is heralded as the future of television with the Government committed to switching off analogue transmission by 2010. DTT doesn't require a satellite dish or decoding technology to view programmes, and offers a range of free-to-air channels including BBC Choice and BBC4. Disadvantages, however, include, the limited number of channels that it can receive (under 30), and the patchy signal at present
Digital versatile disc (DVD)	stores music, video, films and graphics in a digital format. When these are played on a DVD player or home computer the reproduction of sound and image is meant to be near perfect
Drum machines	enable the programming of beats and the eradication of 'mistakes'. A strict temporal grid can be constructed to allow for audio symmetry and musical repetition, but also for an uneven patterning in sound – something 'real drummers' would find very hard to replicate in 'live' performance
Electronic news gathering (ENG)	has radically altered the way news is reported, transmitted, edited and presented on television. From virtually anywhere in the world, location-recorded footage can be computer edited on site, and through a either a satphone (a telephone that has a very small umbrella-like satellite dish connected to it) or a satellite newsgathering unit, news can be uplinked to the news HQ instantaneously to go on air 'live' as is arrives
Full immersion experience	one that bombards, assaults and utilises almost all the senses of the body through a new media device. For example, with electronic games, players are asked to feel the game as they play (PlayStation's 'Dual Shock' controller sends vibrations into the hand-set), believe the game is real (amazing three-dimensional, real time graphics, with coherent narratives, supported by digital, surround sound), and interact with and control the game cerebrally (game players are presented with puzzles, enigmas, pathways and quests that they have to solve to progress in the game)
Global Village thesis	suggests that because of the new media people across the world can communicate and interact with each other in instantaneous exchanges. Consequently, the whole world feels like it has shrunk and that people now live in a 'global village'
Home Computers	multimedia workstations that have transformed the way people work, take part in leisure and entertainment activities, educate and inform themselves about the world, and the way finance and commercial activities can be undertaken
Hyperreality	a theoretical term used to suggest that we are living in an image-world based on simulacra or copy, and where, as a consequence, real, first-hand experiences are replaced by re-presentation, so that the image-screen becomes *more* real than the real itself
Internet	a global network of inter-linked computers that provide users with information, communication and entertainment
Internet Service Provider (ISPs)	connects users or 'subscribers' to the Internet
Hypertext transport protocol (http)	a Web navigational tool which enables the standardised transmission of email, audio and video files between users/computers

IMAX	combines a horizontally-run 70mm film with screen size as large as 100ft x 75ft. The screen itself is slightly curved and with seating arranged in closer proximity, the screen image literally hovers over the audience. This sensory experience is extended through the development of 3D IMAX, where the '3D' glasses that are worn by the audience render the image (film) 3-dimensional
The Information Society Thesis	suggests that the processing, storage, and transmission of all kinds of information are a major feature of the modern world. Through the use of new media and information technologies not only is information everywhere but it is of paramount importance to the way people communicate with each other, learn about the world and to the way they conduct business at home and abroad.
Invisible special effects	constitute up to 90 per cent of the work of the special effects industry and are not meant to be noticed (as special effects) by film spectators as they watch the action/drama unfold
MIDI (musical instrument digital interface)	enables various instruments to be digitally connected up, allowing composition to take place within a computer's memory without the need for those instruments (musicians) to be 'playing' in a 'live' studio space. This means that studio quality recording no longer needs the studio space to produce it – digital signals (different parts of a song, vocals, instrumentation) can be transmitted over distances using both satellite and fibre-optic technology
Mobile phones	transformed the nature of one-to-one communication. Today, no matter where one is – on a train, shopping, out walking, or eating a meal – one can be contacted and can contact someone else with such a device
MTV	the first 24 hour music video station, launched in America in 1981 with a programme consisting of album-orientated rock, chart hits, and the latest releases from the biggest named artists of the time. Over the course of its development this programming has extended out to having stations dedicated to playing particular music genres (mirroring American radio formats), for example MTV2 is dedicated to playing alternative and independent rock/pop, and to having 'regional' differences in what is played, for example MTV Latin America shapes its programming for the local market place.
Multi-User-Domains (MUDs)	online, networked, text-based computer programmes that allow participants to interact with each other in virtual, often fantasy based environments. The MUD interface is a window or portal into another world, where game players take on roles that they script and construct for themselves.
New media	those media technologies (for example the home computer, digital television) and media forms (such as PlayStation electronic games) that are historically recent in terms of invention, entry into the marketplace, and into everyday use
New media texts	are supposedly marked by real interactivity, an abundance of special effects, an increase in visual stimulation and by an exhilarating speed in delivery. Internet game playing would be one example of this highly visual, immediate and interactive experience
Postmodernism	suggests that the new media have radically changed the way people experience and live in the world today. It is argued that through the digitalisation of film, video and television, the development of the multimedia format, and the virtual reality of the Internet and gaming devices, people can no longer tell the difference between reality and fiction, and actually prefer 'hyperreality'.

Showscan	combines the large screen format of IMAX with synchronised, moving and tilting seats in the auditorium
Surveillance cameras	Generally perched on steel posts 5-10 metres above ground, on moveable heads, the surveillance camera ensures that public spaces are kept under 24 hour supervision
The Surveillance Revolution	implies that the new media have been responsible for putting people under almost constant surveillance. Whether at home or at work, shopping or clubbing, driving or travelling by public transport people are being filmed by security cameras, are having information about them stored without their knowledge, and are contactable by phone, fax, email, bleeper, pager, 24 hours a day
Synthesisers	enables sounds to be recorded and stored in a random access memory, manipulated and modified and then retrieved for mixing. Songs emerge from this replication, reproduction and structuring of sound, beat, melody, rather than from the playing or the organisation of 'real' (guitar, drum, piano, etc.) instrumentation
Virtual communities	exist on the Internet and evolve from bulletin-board systems (BBSs), where members of the community leave and retrieve messages, photographs, digital images; 'publish' reviews, statements, arguments, ascribe and demarcate roles, and agree common aims and objectives (for those communities that are goal orientated)
Virtual Reality (VR)	a computer generated, fully interactive, sensory based multimedia environment where the user/player gets to see, feel, hear and move around in a three-dimensional virtual world
Visible special effects	those special effects which produces the 'Wow! That can't be real' reaction from spectators and audiences. The digitally created dinosaurs in *Jurassic Park* (1993) or the stop-motion action-spectacle sequences in *The Matrix* (1999) are two recent examples of this
Web sites	topic/theme based environments found on the World Wide Web
World Wide Web	an interconnected set of computers on the Internet that all use the same communications programme. Web users communicate through what is known as hypertext transport protocol (http)